Honey Dew

by

Darren J Beaney

Contents

LET YOUR HEART DANCE

I fell in love the first time we danced - an uncoordinated
cack-handed avalanche. You bounced over on the balls
of your fine feet and climbed on, staying put, as coy as a well-heeled
sassy lap dancer. My heart started drumming a repetitive beat,

marvellous manic melody. I was blinded by your groovy
glistening glitterball eyes. Felt the fever of your twinkling
Travolta smile. I took the lead resembling a playful lovelorn
puppy. My first left foot kicked my second left foot and we began

to get busy, tumbling toward one another. Shaking, rattling
and rolling, upsetting the rhythm with our rudeness. Showing little
regard for tempo or decorum, neglecting our manners,
we made our own moves as I pulled you

close. Beating up the upbeat as we wrestled and submitted
to an arse pinching smoochathon. We crashed the party, burning
up the rave, intensifying the heat of the latest sizzling tunes.
Gyrated like an uninhibited spin dryer on its last

legs until I buckled against your vibrating
thighs. The lasting effect of our disco damage choreographed
the steps of our destiny. As we gasped
without resting and kissed without breathing and fell without landing.

HONEY DEW

Her sweet smile
clogged
my pulmonary veins.

A smile that cascaded love,
tempted with low hanging kisses
ripe and ecstatic.

A smile I absorbed
as it caressed weakness,
wrapped things up,
left the night   tongue tied.

PLAYING BANJO ON BRIGHTON BEACH

I showed you my banjo
nearly twice our combined age.
It had been through the wars.

I bought it the day before
from a toothless busker
bleating rain weary songs.

It carried countless memories
in the circular membrane
made from battered water buffalo.

Although missing the middle string,
it didn't lament the songs it played.
Folk stories remembered in ivory frets.

I serenaded you with Armenian love
songs composed for ukulele.
Ballads penned in unspun wool
by a love strung young shepherd.

I plucked up the courage
to ask if you played, you replied
all fingers and thumbs.
I put down my banjo on the shingle.

I reached for your thumbs and fingers,
nestled them against my belly,
telling you that you were leading
a soulful band of butterflies.

You fancied my interpretations.
I left an impression with my warbles
as you took a shine to my strumming
and I sang with the setting sun.

FIRST DATE MERRY-GO-ROUND

*The past woke from a rotating slumber
and the world heard it ask to be forgotten.*

He speaks a language heard at punk rock recitals, reserved for eccentrics
and absent academics. He sports an illiterate haircut, dressing
as if old clothes are the sum of a fresh imponderable equation.
She beams all halo, winking at him with a blinding devilish glimmer.
She glides, interesting, captivating - kicking arse in daring dancing boots.

*The buzz took over ways of walking, tales of talking
sights for seeing, the tune of thinking.*

The mares and stallions eventually gallop
into a mix of golden embers - part dozing sun,
a bit waking moon. The enticing shingle has cast its songs and poems.
Another match made, a very real adventure set to begin.

*And he knows what comes next.
If he tells her, will she agree?*

LET'S START SOMETHING WE WON'T WANT TO FINISH

Come and join me! Let's connect.
Be versatile bubbles engrossed in steamy
bathtubs, luscious luxury in thrilling union,
forever finding the fit of each other's fancy and structure.

We'll rule the long dark streets in the small hours
taking our pick of after-midnight gardens. Finding
new territories, reclaiming old favourites.
Bossing the scene, a hot urban fox and cool country vixen.

Let's learn to dance - foxtrot, tango.
Drink cheap whiskey. I'll sweep you off your heels and collect
your falling blushes. When I have them all we will paint
our town, leaving our mark, creating a legend
bigger than Terry & June.

Let's take tea at the Ritz. I'll get dressed up
to the nines with odd socks and no shoes. I'll nibble the crusts
from your sandwiches and blow
like a baby's whisper to cool your brew. You can slurp from your saucer
while I protect you from those uptight stares. When we leave we'll take all the cakes.

Let's occupy grand houses and start
our own cult. I promise to cling to your gospels, and we can gossip
freely with affection. I will find daily kindling
for your lazy rituals. We'll wake each morning to fallen angels
and an eternal love powered by the energy of three chord guitar riffs.

FINDING THE FIT OF EACH OTHER

I saw her soul framed by the glaze
of the spice window. My sight seasoned
by the excitement of her glowing zest. Her eyes
dashing, sclera bright as fresh snow
with blizzard blue irises.   She uttered

a smattering of words, I heard the language
of love and dashed to catch her flurry
of fancy lyrics before they settled
on the cobbles of another dead
end street.   I held my giddy gaze firmly

fixed to zing of her lustre
and skipped around and behind the pane.
I wheezed, breathed hard on the shaking sheet
of spice window. Determined to keep her
hot hint in my eyeline.   Tracing the pizzazz of her shape

on the glass in her exciting fog, using
my trembling finger. She turned, moving
her index tip in delayed union to mine,
learning my outline and we both
discovered we fit
perfect, together.

NOW IT MAKES SENSE

My synapses have yet to shrink back to size
My eyes hang
                                                    ache
My nose has hints of success seasoned with sherbet lemons
My ears wail to the sound of shrill hand bells wielded by wild folk
My mouth is dry   a parched patch of earth in the hottest of summers

The hair on my neck buzzes and boogies   bought to life by high voltage
                    did I step on the Bakerloo Line?

My spine still sustains a seismic shiver
My pulse is more erratic than plans for Brexit
My feet rival Mandela's dance of triumph
My heart vibrates violently   before   barrelling over
                                                        the f
                                                            a
                                                            ll
                                                              s
My palms are itchy   beaded   slippy
          I keep my fingers crossed as I slide my hand into yours

32 *to the power of 22*

Thirty-two birthdays until
the realisation finally
hit home. Thirty-two candles lit.
Thirty-two blown.
Thirty-two New Year's drunk wasted
resolutions. Thirty-two cold
Christmas dinners, cracker hats torn,
repeated jokes and last laugh heart stinging
indigestion. Thirty-two years
on this revolving chance of rock,
just clinging on, before you were sighted.
Thirty-two years and then
the exposure of your stunning
twenty second revelation.

AND SHE SAID

The first time I heard her utter those two words,
my outside world instantly started to curl
& spiral. I asked if she wanted to dance -
she did and my head went into a salsa,
my heart still mambos. She said them again
when I asked her to join me on the pebbles,
where we fell in love
with the idea of cheerily chasing rings around
our fiery verses of Mayday affection, in time to the beat
of the promenade merry-go-round. I am sure
the next moment she said those words is marbled
into her memory. My dashing question eager
to interrupt the adverts of Countdown,
my calculated timing mattered,
hoping her response would work out well.
Resulting in her words
being repeated later that year - a cornelian
red-letter August afternoon posing as a windswept
attention-grabbing Autumnal occasion. Those words,
her words that will live with me always, eternal
until the reaper chooses their exclamation.
However, until we are parted, she always
turns to me at night, in our homespun bed
& waves a wispy kiss at my cheek,
desiring that I have sweet dreams.
Still willing to please I embrace
my opportunity to say those words back,
so,   she gets to hear

    I will.

STILL FALLING IN LOVE

My shoelaces flutter silently, tickled by a spring
breeze, inspiring my delighted feet to dance.
Frivolous drizzle cleanses, nurtures a purified
honest veneer, drying and shining in the alluring
sun. Sincere rays reach with warm touch toward the rain,
cheering, easing, encouraging
it to play and parade on pastures new.
I breathe in the party
and air oozes from my lungs, full of promise.
Tasting true, immediate.

YOU AND ME, US TWO

Our love is driven by neat engines of persistence
shuddering to the twitch of our touch, firing the luscious
laughter and locomotion of a lifespan together.

Our single-minded ambition is the recipe
for romance. Our hearts are twisted into love knots, like fresh
pretzels baked with tenderness, brushed with strawberry jam kisses.

Our warmth is our bond. Our relationship simple
as a new Puritan. Sustained without effort, lazy,
as wonderful as bunches of late May daffodils.

Our passion is as exciting as Caxton's
very first page, printed with a love song for Cupid. Each day
is Valentine's Day stuffed into our Christmas stocking.

Our affection is perfect, a hug and antidote
to a processed low regard world that whirls and pivots
in modern angst of mistreated promises and ruined dreams.

Our union, our glorious smudge of life,
the mark we leave on this realm,
floats on sun drenched glitter clouds of confident hope.

Our trust, our fabulous friendship
is a composition fit to be played
in the magnificent memories of our wedding.

ROOT AND BRANCH

Still germinating deep within the soil
of my soul, growing strong like an ancient oak.
Roots spreading through my emotions,
flourishing like a mighty Sequoia.

My heart pumps vital affection, like sap
nourishing our common desire. As tenderness
grows, my feelings branch out to you. Sonnets
and melodies blossom each year, birds and bees
frolic and feast on our fragrant nectar.

My fingers are fine twigs softly touching your face.
My leaves rustle gently in a summer meadow breeze when we kiss.
My feelings make their mark each day,
gaze deep inside at the ever-expanding circle of growth rings.

My passion is a thing of splendour to observe.
My desire as strong as Mahogany.
Our initials are carved in the bark
for all to see. The magnitude of my love
reaches from the end of the deepest root
to the tip of the very broadest branch.

CHASING HER & THE PLANETS

Relentless, like storm's gale.
Only summer sunlight
burns warmer.   So beautiful!

Akin to evening moon   &   morning
blossom.

I run through the universe
look to her shining star
out with planets.

& I tell my secret.

Yelling.
    Lost in reverie
    never whisper my love for her!

PORRIDGE, MY LOVE

The smoke detector sensed I was hoping for a sneaky Sunday
snooze in. The shrill siren soon saw to that, my sly shut eye
and piles of snoring zzz's snatched from my sweaty clutches.
I had been stuck fast, sandwiched between the sheets
and sweet dreams of sweltering sun-soaked festival floats, sultry seas
and sixty-six shipwrecked squid having a whale of a time,
a jolly old knees up, celebrating my birthday, singing silly shanties
and sinking skip loads of Sangria.
I was left scratching and stretching, breaking the surface,
squeezing daylight from my eyes.

As the startling wailing subsided another sleepy sense
stirred from its slumbers. Burnt bacon wafted my way.
For some non-meat eaters, the stink of rashers and rind
is torment, a wind up, a reminder of shamefaced pleasures
long since passed. Not me, all I could smell was the scorched
skin of scorn. But soon a new scent, the subtle hint of porridge,
shrewdly drifted toward my prone olfactory neurons, skipping
seductively toward the most suitable synapse.

Despite feeling sluggish in my somnolent state, I knew
that this was a signal of love, a sign of serious affection. My sweetheart
showing a singular devotion, a desire to please, sending
me a birthday message, a secret code of significance that speaks
volumes, the size of which I simply shudder at. Because we both know
that porridge is a secret symbol of our love. It is unhurried, inspired,
soaked with simple effort, scores formidable results. It is steady and consistent
a safe bet that satisfies. It is the glue that holds us together, the sweet
steaming substance that sustains and binds. Stuffed to the splitting seams with
splendidness.
We could spread it on our palms and our held hands would be stuck fast for eternity.

Her choice of sautéed fried staples suggests she too has a poetic, romantic side.
The golden perfectly formed yolk is the setting sun shining on the secluded
sandy shore, on the first night of our Spanish honeymoon. The beans
and brown sauce show her love of the variety and spice of life. The subtle spread
of slightly salted butter on crisp seeded toast echoes the touch of her slender
fingertips on my shivering spine. The freshly squeezed Saville orange juice
makes our hearts sing, and she leads the sing-along chorus of our lovely song.
The scalding cup of freshly brewed coffee tastes succulent, the strong aroma
seeps into my pores. The caffeine hit and the slap of the food rush gives us
the energy, the oomph, the verve to build up a head of sizzling steam,
and we shuffle smugly and suggestively back to bed.

THIS IS A LOVE SONG

I want to write
you a love song.
A poem of affection
and pure adoration.
Full of my feelings
for you. But
my love
for you is
ineffable!

THE COLOUR OF OUR LOVE

Orange
is the colour of our love.

Our time scattered with orange rays
of X-rated morning glory sunrise, provoked from comfort
by curvy peaches. So perky that sanity
becomes overripe and spews, dripping
melted orange seed over our unwrapped seams
and piles of so blatantly discarded orange stitches.

Orange
we exclaim!
Orange we sing. Our buzz of union.
As one
we reach out for the shaft of orange
joy.

Orange is the colour of us, beaming and fertile. Ripe
like All Hallows pumpkins, as succulent as the flesh
of our very first shared kumquat. Hot and exotic.
Sweet and fiery,
yet not made for sharing. The orange glow
on our palette is a perfect mix.
Conceived for our pure indulgence,
for our memories only.

Orange
our beacon. Colour that mimics our lust.
Orange
flow of our lives, shade of our laughter.
Orange
flavour of our love, shape of our affection.
Sweet, sometimes sticky.

Satisfying
like a carton bursting
with orange
Smarties.

EVENING IN

You have worked your wine glass so hard
it is now exhausted.
You cast it aside.
The twinkle in your eye has a knowing look of sage about it.
Visibly cosy.   You grin.

You lean my way, littering my ear
with a litany of frivolously pinpointed words,
hinting that you desire a steamy night.
You indulge by opening a new bottle,
waving a whiff of seduction under my nose

and in a slowly sloshed manner
pour yourself a long relaxing bubble bath.
You enthusiastically abandon your clothes
and pencil in a rendezvous with me in an hour, perhaps two,
as you sashay serenely into Radox indigo effervescence.

You let your smooth skin soak away,
welcoming ripples and crinkles
that wash over you, leaving behind
a newly laundered corrugated complexion.

And when you have had your fill
of humidity, dampness, of being so moist.
Can take no more of the wetness,
can no longer be bothered with lather,

you resurface, for the encore.
Turning out an enticing entrance,
in a flourish of tantalising towelling.
Drip, drip, dripping on the parquet floor,
each drop reflecting you and your night time radiance.

To cap things off we share a special brew.
Hurray for Horlicks!   Bravo for bed!
I anticipate page turning passion,
but you are snoring with all of your heart
before the first line is even uttered.

AMOROUS QUERIES

When Eros asks his thought-provoking questions
where can I go for answers?

The corners of your soul? The uncharted
places in your existence? The contours
of your skin, the confluences of your bones?
How about the folds of your hands or the tips
of your fingers?   Stretched to make the point.

Can I trace the twitching of your nerves or follow
the crisscross of veins, a love map
to the peripherals of your heart?   Where
the faintest beats mean the most.   Can I catch
clarification in your stuttering
breath as your lungs labour under the weight
of affection? Will I spot
it in the twinkle in your homely eyes?   So honest.

Or grasp the solution in your sweet smile?
That speaks volumes, curious, at times double Dutch.
Perhaps hear enlightenment in the roar
of your body language and gain complete
understanding in the feedback of your touch?

SURFIN' GIRL

The blue haired girl once surfed through the park,
secure in her fashion. Floodlit eyes
shining on improbable catwalks,
parading her tone. Inflating the hearts
of those she invited to climb on her board.

Rinsing aqua to blond, nothing dumb
in that, her glow radiated
like polished platinum, leaving
an iridescent trail so precious
that he followed adventurous,
trekking. His quest to collect all her smiles.

Then au natural, stunning brunette
radiant like her eyes that sparkled
brighter with each tide. Rousing, she added
to the understanding of many, multiplying
knowledge, explained the value of π,
leaving memories that cannot be taken away.

Now with a few hairs of grey she leads
as a mother. Inspiring! Her love
is uncomplicated with no rules
and she cares. Her love is like oceans,
her affection forever gently lapping against our shores.

In years still to come she may be white
like teachers' chalk. She may change colour
again to mask the signs of passing years.
But she will never disguise what is inside,
she will always ride the waves like
the blue haired girl.

PHOTO BOOTH

Is our love real? Really
true? We have never posed in a tight fit
photo booth. We have no sticky
streamer of passport size pictures – glossy
silly postures.   Puckered pouts,   protracted kisses.
Fumbling with one eye open,   checking the exposure.

SNAP!

   Without the evidence how do I know
if it is what you truly testify to?
My love...

THE MISSING BIT

I can't shake the feeling
that there is never enough
And that I don't show you

and that I don't   convince you

    And that is the bit
      that is missing

And I want our love to mean
 as much as Dr King's dream
with as much passion
 as a catalogue of first kisses

because we are so much more
than love bites and candlelight

SALUTATIONS

To mum and dad xx
To Ben, Lucas and Jazzmin xxx
To Tobias, Link, Ace and Malachai   xxxx

To Esme and Ollie xx xx

To my friends who share my love

With thanks to -
Mark Hedgehog for making this pamphlet happen

Matt Bemment for the wonderful cover design

John McCullough for inspirational teaching
Jess Moriarty for wonderful constructive feedback - can you see the
changes

Alan Meggs and Barbara my MA buddies and critical friends who have
read so many of my poems and many versions of the ones seen here -
Cheers you two

To everyone who has ever attended Flight of the Dragonfly

Finally,
 this collection is dedicated to **Joanna** who I love with every molecule I
possess
and with every word in these poems xxx

DJB
November 2020